Sandpaper

Patrick Green

erbacce-press
Liverpool UK

5 Farrell Close, Melling, Liverpool, L31 1BU, UK

erbacce-press publications Liverpool UK 2021

erbacce-press.co.uk
ISBN: 978-1-912455-25-6

Acknowledgements

Thank you so much to everyone who has encouraged and supported me over the years:

Ms Chambers (for putting up with me), all the rents, family and close friends (you know who you are) and my wife (for listening to me and loving me for who I am).

A big thank you to Dr Alan Corkish/*erbacce*-press for giving me the opportunity to share my work with more people.

Finally, thank you to those who read these poems.

Dedicated to Mouse

Index

Earth Man

I search for who
I am in
the woods
behind the
house
that does
not
belong to me.

Garden Visit

The blue of my jeans
tricks him into believing
that I am one more flower
in the garden.

Bonjour papillon.

Strong winds helped
break him free
from a world
of darkness.

How do I know all this?

Because he whispered it
to me,
after sensing
I had a heart beat.

America

No Entry

Glowing in
Red

The pathway is
Wide open

If only I dared
To disobey
The sign

Either way I should
Regret nothing.

Graveyard: Song 1

The sky is a circular
window.

It scratches at
my throat.

I think of escape, but
I always
knew…

…that the crows would
play kiss chase on
white stones.

Like a humourless
piano, sending
out discordant
notes.

How the world
could come to
this:

Swinging in
diagonals…

…hanging in
blue and green.

Caught by a Nuclear Wave

Drowned in ancient history.

Book ruin,
built as a temple
of destruction.

Black ink symbols,
fading to
blotched blue prints.

Pity pouring from the red sun sky
and grinding all to a halt.

Not a Soldier

What is it that you're waiting for?

A ringing phone,
a bang on the door

or are you longing
to see,
what you
once saw,
so many days

behind.

What pleasure is it that you seek?
To make the world seem less bleak?

Will you only watch?

Or can you speak,
of what is coming next?

These prison walls,
this white washed town,
with no purpose
or warning sign.

Slowly

fading all the while.

A face sad in
the mirror.

What way now is the best?
A riverside,
where you

can rest.

Still on your
own with all that's left.

Empty hands that hurt.

And from the picture
you step out,
but the film keeps rolling round,
and all the pages
full of doubt,

they never really

helped

you out.

The people now create a pile.
It really does not make a smile,

for only

hopefully

in a short while,
you will be
moving
on.

What do you think?

A cluster of white men
wearing suits,
smart ties, smart shoes
clean-shaven, short hair.
In a large room.

Creating a spiralled
chain link with their
bodies.

Their heads slightly bowed, their eyes all closed
their mouths muttering words.
Looking on I admire their actions.

One suited man
then appears before me
in front of the gathering.

I welcome him
and his eyes
appear at first clear.
He comes closer,

they become
two pools
of darkness.

He grabs me.

I now understand.

I struggle to get away.
My mouth stuck.
As much as I try
my jaw will not be released.
I scream inside
my mind,
using the sentence I know will
free me.

Your hand sweeps into view.

I am awake.
I tell you
what I've witnessed.

Tell Me

What's it like

To hear the steam
From a coffee maker

The chatter from each
Table and corner

The sound of change
Clinking in the register

The ring and arrival
Of another smiling
Stranger

?

What's it like

To sit opposite a friend
Or two

To pat a back

To shake a hand

To stand shoulder to shoulder whilst
Helping with a coat for
The back of
A chair

?

What's it like

To break from routine

To taste a sandwich made
By someone else

To drink tea from an
Unusual cup

?

What's it like

To watch the street
Behind glass

People crossing
Each other's
Paths

?

What's it like

To be under
The sky that's blue
And the clouds that are white

And to not notice
How they are moving
And where they are heading

?

What's it like

To have one more stir
With a spoon

And to place it on
An unused
Saucer

?

What's it like

To
Breathe
With each
Other

?

Odd Trip

Slow moving vehicle.
Hogging up the road.
Crawling on its pointless path.

Big and yellow.

Wide and imposing.
Dragging a trail of bored faced passengers
in it's wake.

In the upper room

(Previously published by *Vonnegut Collective*; 2020)

I look up and through the skylight.
I am a fish in a bowl without water.

The world is blue.
The tree over the rooftop is green,
Its leaves are notes upon growing staves.
They wave at each other.
They are unstoppable.

I hear the wind through the branches,
And the occasional sound of birds.
It all finds its way through the gaps.

Downstairs the rumble of a washing machine
And the gurgle of pipes disturbs my
Meditation.

I cannot help but let the thought creep in =
Real life is out there.
I am in here, a body upon a carpet.

The threads become barer each day.

What happened in a London café?

The sound of their voices
cutting up my thoughts.
Thoughts of love
and unity.
Thoughts of peace
and tranquillity

I try to drink my tea
and sit being me.
Perfectly in harmony
or at least trying to be.

Their voices at first noise,
I let in.
I let it be distraction.
The noise forms words.
These words express.
Their inner concerns,
their inner worries.

I try to block the words
from taking root within
my mind.
For surely body and
spirit would follow.

I'd feel the need
to act
in line

with what
they say.

The man says:

“I worry what will happen after
2020.”

The woman nods in agreement.
Does he know something I don’t?
What is the significance of this number?

It looks friendly written down.
To worry is to sin.

And so I let their conversation
turn to mud.

A language without
words, a noise
and then sludge.

My tea tastes good
and smells good
and I am joyful -
with my thoughts
of love and unity.
Thoughts of peace
and tranquillity.

Carefree

One hand
holding a branch
to steady himself,
the other holding a blade.

Carving a line.
Finishing a fresh
statement -

'The world is flat'

Sap falling from the tips of the letters.

His rucksack -

full of rocks, speckled in a multitude of colours,
made the descent more difficult.

A swarm of black bees swayed in unison
down the mountainside.
They projected their humming all the way to his insides.

…

A light bulb burnt out in a lamp on his old
boyhood desk.

His mother stopped looking for ways
to hold his internal turmoil
in her own skull a few days before passing.

The bulb had gone warm amber.
Smoke rolled around the glass bubble
sweetly kissing the cold sphere.

He need not dwell on such sentimentality – bulbs
and desks and mothers
weren't needed in the open air.

At last -

To smell the pines
to watch the sky

and dance in the river
with a knife.

Vancouver

(Previously published in *The Cannon's Mouth*; June 2012)

Covered in post-it notes, covered in paper scraps
and metal clips.
Held together with masking tape.
Blu-tac merging with fabric

and skin.

Wild beard with wild eyes and fading wispy hair.
Ranting and waxing, pouring advertisements
onto the avenue crossroads.

It's sad to watch him trying to sell
the words he scribbles down.

Rushing from person to person.
Every time being ignored.

He points and demands

"I'll write one for you sir, I have one for you ma'am"

It's been this way for so long.

Then when the paper is turned down he tacks it to an empty space
or covers up an old note more likely.

He's a dripping ink yeti.

If they cleared him of his letters,
they'd find he were just a ghost underneath.

Poor, delicate and always desperate.

Where does he spend his evenings and time off?
Does he type continuously without a break?
Does his mind ever stop?

I wonder if the lines he writes,
are priceless beyond measure.

The Wish

(Previously published in *erbacce;* 2019)

It's behind the T.V
in the wires that are crossed and ending
at the plugs.

It's on a fish hook
getting pulled and acting like the wind
round a corner and up a back alley
ending in the alley bin behind the pizzeria.

It's just slithered the length of a pavement and slicked into a park.

Now it's with the bread crumbs
floating on the duck pond.

It's travelling the metro line.
It's drowning in a sea of stuffy heat

on the back row of the number 23.

It's whispered within a prayer
that's waiting for a reply.

It's always one step in front.
Teasing and playing and laughing
on the railings and the swinging overhead telephone cables.

It looks out of all the windows and
It ends with yet another.

The Mountain

I've felt the feet
Of many souls
Digging into me

Their hands have
Run across my face

Their fingertips have
Clung desperately
To my edges

I've been looked
At with awe

I know abandonment
I know perseverance
I know the view from
My top
Will show you the
World

When out of sight
I live in the spirit
Of the boy who's
Dreams never cease

I am the witness of
The sun
Falling and
Rising.

Sometimes

Sometimes it's the small things that move us
Like a kiss in the rain
Like a hug in the rain

Sometimes it's the big things that move us
Like a lightning storm
Or the ground that shakes

Sometimes it's insignificance that moves us
Like the words on a page
or the flutter of a bird.

The Rat

Feeling like god again
the man in the white overalls
prods his experiment slave
through a wire cage.

Which sits in the centre of a white sanitized room
where everything but the cage
and his utensils are white.

It's an alien environment.
But necessary,
of course.

These Words

These words
Can build you up

These words
Can bring you down

These words
Can get you above the clouds

These words
Can send you under the ground

These words
Can get you through a wall

These words
Can make the whole wall fall

These words
Could form a song to sing

These words
Could mean everything.

Mr

Bank holiday Monday.
Hope you're happy old man.

Alone at the dinner table.
Supping copious amounts of bad coffee
in a standard cup

and taking little time on deciding
what next to eat alone.

My pity reaches you unnoticed.
I should have just got up
and sat down opposite you.

You'd probably be offended.
Whether your sadness could fill
the Pacific or not in reality who knows?
But it shines a light on mine regardless.

Observation on humanity

Many people believe
they are more important
than other people.

This creates a lot
of problems.

A Coin

Behold an English tragedy
Two factions of society

Some that do
And some that don't
Some that will
And some that won't.

Who was the first doctor?

(Previously published in *Neon Highway;* 2009)

Twisting and agitated, shuffling, mumbling
the doors await a new heaven to face.

A floral dress, a smile
shimmers and disappears.
All confusion dream state,
dead or alive now who's to know?

Sterile, clinical room adult conversation.
Ignored for awhile then 'Hello, friend!'
Have a drink,
onto your suit.
The walls are creepers without moving.
Want to reach for the corners and
escape, this block has no exits.
Talk, talk, blank fill, blank fill,
off and on, hot cold, here now, gone then.
Lie down, stay still, pinch skin,
Mum, dad, blurred.
In God's league?

They've come to pack for the next life.
Floating wish suspended, see the situation
from a diamond perspective.

Reality zero, reality what.
Pull the threads and rip the curtain.
Under and out.
Please help you're hurting me.

Future use the power people in those fists.
For the walls are melting, feet bleeding.
The grass trying to run, slowing down.

Page illuminating bedroom,
spectacles leaning over the morning after.
A rare entrance to embrace.
Stones thrown as hard as possible
across an empty farmer's field.
Start of making sense of all the pills.

Boyhood Wasteland

You're a wire of a man,
thin and in places sharp with little spikes.
Try to climb over the fence

…and there you are, wire of a man.
Ugly grey and barbed.
In sections overlapping.
Over the top you'll snag our t-shirts
and jeans and tear long lines down the material bought
or handed down to us.

…and we will laugh at first
…and then try to run,
but the fun won't last.

When one escapes and the other has been caught.

Short legs flapping a few feet above the ground,
whilst another pair heads up an escape route.

Your metal fingers clawing him back.
Scolded with ranting,
battered into saying sorry.

All we did was climb there was no other motive.

The T.V tower watching the entire incident
under its frame.
To it we're the same.

Wire boys and wire man.

Beast Clothes

We are the clothed animals.
Washed and ready to do whatever we are told,
in a civilized and orderly manner.

We must not cause a scene
or make a spectacle of oneself.
Polite, patient and smiling
at all times.

But get us in the dark,
within our private lives,
within our private minds,
and we snarl and snap and wail
and whimper and cry and crumble.
We roam free from constraint and direction
and dance around open fires.

Then we awake as the caged animals,
re-apply the shackles and throw away the keys.

Jackets of Dead Men

Retro store
it reads - step in for consumerism interests.

Trinkets and once posh porcelain
floods every shelf.
Dust even gathers in the fingernails of the shop owner.

There's a flogged fox fur.
There's a suitcase full of forgotten war medals.
There's a penny-farthing cracked bike seat
and a faded British flag scrunched up like a used kitchen flannel.

Women's Victorian black in mourning dresses up on plastic hangers,
mini-melodramas of infant fatalities wept over.

All under one roof.

Now a back room.
A long row of tweed and elbow patches, a brass button
and a frill of tassels in gold.

Grey, black, brown organized in size.
All for sale, old tired and worn-out.

Can make out hands and heads and legs, standing in a cue.
No thanks a new jacket would be better.

Freaking out over a line of death.
Can see the shop owner poaching jackets of the backs of deceased OAPs,
sneaking into homes through vegetable plots and garden gates.

Skulking around a naval ship rocking on the ocean.
Waiting for the captain to be killed by a Spanish fleet relentless canon fire.
So she can peel the blood stained garment from his limp frame,
pop it in on an eighty wash and sell alongside other kitsch items
to unsuspecting fashion searchers.

Check Out

I'm in the library.
The library where he worked.
The library where he used to stack the shelves
quietly with the books.

It is mid week and it's un-full.
Maybe the time he hated most.
When all he had was stacking books,
and being with his thoughts.

Hollow kind eyes, distant far off smile.
A friendly man without friends.

I did not really know him.
A background character,
slotted in alphabetically.

Almost easy to miss
amongst the other authors.

He didn't walk, he slowly shuffled.
Never picked his feet up.

His back was slightly bent,
from centuries of book lifting.

From the backroom with all the
older paperbacks and hardbacks.
Speckled with dust and musty mold,
he came and went.

From the library each day,
he came and went.

Working and growing weaker,
smiling less
each hour that passed.

The life he led,
It came and went.

Childish Games

That game we used to play as youngsters,
a personal favourite.

Round the edges of your room.
Swinging from wardrobe door
to desk.
Clambering on shelves and bouncing across the bed.
Edging upon the windowsill.
Stepping on a chair and off a chair.

Laughing when it all went wrong.
As one of us or both of us
would tumble to the floor
in a heap.
Hair muffled and clothes askew.

If you hit the deck,
or even slightly felt it, you were out,
and the whole room had to be circulated.

Now I'm older
I find myself in most situations
still trying
not to touch the floor
and yet I touch it much more than I used to.

Every step in fact.

City Living Dream

I dream of gaps in pavements,
alongside new pristine buildings
and clogs of used confectionary wrappers.

I see them still in piles ignored and untouched
by the bristles of stationary street cleaning vehicles.

Gloomily gliding along I touch the cheeks
of stone washed concrete council blocks
and then pass over the concrete crafted connecting bridges.

I catch each face with detail.
They store up in the logbook of my memory,
without effort or concentration.

They appear and fall and slot in place in geometric order.

I dream I walk around like this for days,
without fully appreciating the fact the sun is shining

and two friends passing by sharing a joke,
that I am not included in passing by them.

I dream I am alone, constantly alone,
I hold fast to the sides of my dream, I rip it down,
I pierce it with the tips of my shoes and
screw it up into scraps of unwashed laundry.

Then I sit slightly hollow eyed and sallow coloured
and weary.

Wishing it were just a dream and not an opportunity of reality.

Dave

We walked across
the iron bridge.
It towered above all others.

It made the buildings
down below seem insignificant
and lacking in the ornate.

Whilst we enjoyed
the car fumes and river air,
I surprised him with asking
for a cigarette.

Then we smoked and
continued our journey
from one side to the other.

He told me I smoked like a Nazi.
He said it in between a chuckle.
I'm not sure why he said it,
how does a Nazi smoke exactly?

And even more questionable is David's
knowledge on how one would smoke.

The surreal comment made me laugh.
I'm not easily offended.
We share in the same
bizarre humour.

That and our love for hating
everything and being openly cynical.

The bridge I miss,
The smoking I now do without,

and Dave
he is irreplaceable.

Deane and his family

One two three four five six seven

eight nine ten eleven twelve thirteen fourteen fifteen.

Count them from left to right

Work across then start on the next line

Window, window, window, door, window
balcony stretching long.

His is the bottom row without the view
of the seventies brown brick supermarket.

There's no plastic plants in his window
like the old ladies next door.

He has a younger brother, who looks like him
and a mum and a dad.
They both get their sharp features and dark hair
from both their parents.

Deane came across as nasty at first.
Then his humour came over.
He was fun, a fun character,
With a side order of a challenge.

His mum was quiet and had a sad smile,
his younger brother mimicked her.

You could tell they all looked out for one another.

A happy family truly.

Only Deane's dad did heroin
and that's why they were here.
Window, window, door.

Balcony above them.

New Landing

Like white shark teeth
the mountains sit semi hidden
on the horizon.

Traffic builds up on the
downtown direction side.
It hurts the neck to keep
on watching it.

No one walks,
well rarely on the baking spring pavements.

In the hotel
watching from the bed -
the parking lot,
the splashes of green,
the western world.

Worn out motel signs,
petrol stations,
softly spoken undecipherable accents
behind on the trains that travel through the sky.

Each face unknown.
Many streets unexplored.
Foreign all foreign.
Followed by uneasy feelings and
worn-out paranoia.

Here to try and find meaning, purpose and direction.
Surely what is always longed for.
Written down as a constant.

Whether here or there,
sitting and waiting for life to catch up and begin.

Much the same as the planes that are
dragged through on puppet strings.

The Deepest of Blues

Now that I've had time
To think it through
What is my life
Without you?

A distance that
Cannot be measured
A bucket load
Of memories
Treasured

Now that I've awoken
To a new reality
Very little feels
Real to me

This paperweight
Within my heart
Waiting for
A life to
Start

-

Now all I hear is the
Sound of the clock
Now all I hear is the
Rain on the roof top
Now all I see is the
Numbers rize
Now all I see is the
Shirts and the ties

-

But I could be only confused
I'm walking into
The deepest of blues.

Ode to Phil O

His general knowledge
is phenomenal
due to his long unemployment
and need to prove his intelligence
perhaps to the outside world.

Now he works within a generic centre of town cinema
that's overprized, and the popcorn
comes in too many sizes
with confusing prices.

Very well read from Kerouac to Tolstoy
amongst hundreds of other
difficult to pronounce ancient
Russian writers who people
read simply to drop into conversation,
but Phil reads them mainly
out of loneliness, that's my guess.

He likes to keep it old school.
But ironically listens to

50's and 60's music on compact CD and mp3
rather than record.

A pipe is smoked on occasion
in the kitchen
with a cup of tea
and an old-man flat cap
for effect.

Hasn't had a girlfriend or a boyfriend
since?
Well I'm not sure. High school?
Or maybe he has.

I'd like to see him working
Either in radio.
Failing that he should run
his own cinema.
One with rouge curtains
and spots of gold.
Only one screen though.

Running from Jiles

His blonde hair
blackened by unwashed grease.
His wearing of dribble stained
navy blue jumper.

His awkward shuffling,
sometimes-falling feet.

We ran from him.
We misunderstood him.
We saw our imperfections in him
a little too loudly.

We thanked god for not being him.
We pushed him if he came to close.
We shouted harsh words.
We forgot them as soon as they left our mouths…

…and we laughed when Jiles couldn't handle the concrete stairs.
We wondered why he wasn't the same as all of us,

but we never voiced those thoughts.

Past Couple

This was your favourite spot.
I'm sorry I took it up,
Bill and Ina.

Pigeons haunt
the space under
a tree behind the bench.

White, brown and grey
and purple looking plumage.

It's you they see
not me.

You both hold hands and enjoy the view
of iron bridge,
and changing seasons.

Wings rise into
the horizon and ascend
to heaven.

The names engraved will rot away with the bench.

She

Grab the ties, pull at them hard.
Twist the wooden cross frame in hectic motion.
sway to and fro.

Smack the puppet on the wall.
Watch as it slides down to the floor.

Leave the puppet without direction,
without helping hands.

Take notes down on how
the frail wooden toy can’t make its own decisions.

Be delicate when gluing together its fractured splintered limbs.
Untangle strings, retouch the chipped paintwork with prickling bristles.

Then neglect the slumping puppet by stating its not a toy to touch
just a fireplace ornament to admire.

Vacation

Jesus is alive.
I saw him
in the south of France.

Driving an off cream slightly rusty Escort.
It had beige leather seats lined with seams.
His wife was next to him in the passenger seat.

It's the truth.
He had long waving brown hair
and a scraggly beard.

She had slightly longer brown waving hair.
They had olive complexions and beautiful smiles.

He smiled at me as he pulled out of his parking space
in the old monastery car park.

Then we went down into the cave with a few other tourists
to see the ancient church and the tombs even further below it.

Those cold corridors of which I don't fully remember.
But I do remember seeing Jesus and his wife.

They looked like old-fashioned hippies.
But they were probably only in their late twenties.

No one will believe me,
But I saw and I know
Jesus is alive.

The Time is Right

The time is right
To create
A rhythm
On a drum

The time is right
To make
A fire
And dance
In unison

The time is right
To let
The stars
Shine brighter
Than before

The time is right
To take
The gate
Away
And let in
So much more

The time is right
To plant a seed
And watch
The tree
Grow

The time is right
To share
The land
Let everybody know

The time is right
Choose
What you
Are fighting
Against

The time is right
Strike
Down
Evil
And not sit on
The fence

The time is here
The time is now

Step into the light

The time = is right.

First Thing

Trying not to move the blankets
or bounce the mattress.
Staying as still as possible.

The room encased
in dull not depressing light

And just above the blanket line,
your unblemished soft face,
eye lashes facing downward.

Sleeping into the pillows.
Waiting to be awoken.

In the few minutes
that I am alone,
alive, watching from my side.

Knowing that soon, I'll be the
catalyst of your awakening.

I realize then
I am purely
in love.

Happening

Spindly fingers hold out
there lacking love
into the wind.

For dirt ridden, pretend clean
feather falling pigeons.

They didn't intend to be like this
it just kind of happened.

Slates on red brick houses
slide out of sight,
and into back alleys and waiting
patient drains.

Left with holes and rain and inside puddles.

It wasn't meant to be like this,
it crept up and happened.

Happened for a reason, perhaps in an ordered
overlord pattern.

Indoors sitting at the wood chop,
chewing on burnt offerings
of information.
Whilst dull blue, grey light grows
fatter out.
Causing suffocation.

Low and high and inescapable.

Well you know it just kind of happens.

I Watch

I watch the bumblebees
Do their dance
Amongst the flowers
Around the plants

The small birds visit
They come and go
I try to study them
But I'm too slow

Then I think I've caught
The breeze
But it runs away
Through the trees

Down the hill to the river
Touching its banks
Flowing to a bigger
Water expanse

I take in the sky
It's blue
It's vast
Reminds me of
The future
The present
And the past.

Be

On the horizon
The desert sand drifts
A man in flowing robes of black
Leads a camel
By a rope in his hand

Through a haze of heat he walks
Slow and tall
The sun is so high
His figure casts no shadow

I watch him
From under a rock
It covers my head like a blanket
A child would hide under

I want to join his footprints
And let him lead me to living water

There I could wash of my scales
Grow legs
Have a soul
And be a man.

Warning

Both words and silence
can destroy a person.

Between

Back at the kettle
Click

Cup
Pot
Tea out of cupboard

Spoon out the draw

Wait near the fridge
Wait near the window
Wait near to the table

Burn hand
Now at sink
Cool it

Get a tray

Try not to shake
Try not to
See life
As a
Symptom
Of illness

Drink tea
Watch T.V
Read a book
Then try to sleep.

Inpatient

He does not say his name.
Dust spills over
warm weak light.

Feet make sounds.
A delay
the distance
causes.

It's like a
wall of
air got built.

I can't yet reach him.

From down the corridor,
with early morning in its
windows.

And scraps of painted
nonsense,
waiting for the bin.

Keep on keeping on

One more mile
You have to make
Better not make
Any mistakes

Trip on your lace
Land on your face
That's got to burn
Take another turn

Got holes in your pockets
That's ok, you've got nothing
To put in them

One more boy
One more girl
Just a little more crude
Oil, to the world

Slip on the spill
Hope it don't kill,
That's got to burn
Take another turn.

Library Essential (Public and Central)

They've got books
Any old books
Books to make them
Look at home
In a place so grand

They've got bags
Worn out looking
Bags
Bags full of
Essentials
To get by
To survive

They've got each
Other
One mirroring
The other
They've got time
And their grey hairs
Say they've had some

I'm just the same
Waiting not for
Change
Waiting for a whisper
To lead us out
Of here

Maybe when
It's opening
Maybe
When it's closing
Keep the funding
Coming
We need a place
To sit

We've got books
We can still read
We might not
Be leaving
But in our minds
We leave.

At Night

Out of the darkness
a moth appears,
then fades,
then returns.

It beats its body
against
the glass,
longing
to be in
the light.

What Would You Do?

On a beach of stones
a line of people
wait along the shoreline.

Holding a basket
I pass through
the crowd
and place it into the sea.

A number of indistinguishable
sea creatures
swirl
in the grey shallows.

A small manta ray
finds its way
into my container.

I take it from
the water.

But swiftly
throw it back in.
Having barley lifted it out.

As soon as I do so
a wolf emerges
from under an
incoming low wave
and goes for me.

I turn and break back
through the crowd.

The wolf pursues me…

and I run.

Jigsaw

You stack and sort,
Searching for the pieces

To fill the middle

The lid has a completed
Image - the direction
Head that way

But the pieces
There not all placed yet
The time limit
It is not set

Outside the world
Turns dark blue
And black

Inside you and me and a fire.

Brief Reflection

'That's sad'
we pass by

talking of other
frustrations.

Ignoring the nature
around us.

The rabbit still
time jumps
into my mind.

Eyes open
on its side.

Letting in dreams
of escaping that fox
and skirting that barbed wire fence.

In other days
I would have
held
and placed
in a neatly dug
square.

Even said a prayer.

But everyday
is a funeral now.

Object

The shape is ancient,
made from a tree.
A life taker,
not one to help breath

Mine is metal,
cold,
but still weighted.

I lost the chain
and now
it no longer
hangs from my neck.

But should it have always
been on my back?

It is lost between
discarded objects,
boxes
of shadows
and papers
with scribbles.

But it’s there,
always.

Cold metal,
waiting
to be taken
up.

This Guitar

It’s a used
spade with chips in its
wooden handle
and mud caked over
all its surface.

It’s a relic,
nailed to the inside of a
cave. Its silence
looks like music,
Its strings are dust particles.

Then it’s life -
plugged in
electrified.
It’s lightning
striking
the heels of a fleeing
rabbit.

It’s the covering of a forest path.
Each note a petal
falling from
who knows what tree.
One after another
and then a multitude.

Look back, see the path covered
for another walker
to walk on.

It's a disagreeable
lawyer that can't let go
of the case -
and stays up too late
and wakes up to early.

It's a chance harmony.
A stream starting point,
trickling out a mountain top.

Its got the
holy spirit
working through it
and it wants
to spread its
message of
light through
every ear drum.

Hear it beating.

Don't leave it in
the box.

Accident

A needle
going rusty
in a medical jar.

Left in the back of
a kitchen cupboard.

My name written
in un-neat handwriting -
like the surgeon
had too much on that
week
or perhaps
their hand
hadn't been used.

The writing would
have been immaculate,
you would hope.

A needle, that and my scar
reminds me -

not all play
is harmless.

More Visions

The tornado
Raged
Overhead

Ripping up roots
Removing trees

I found a staff
In my hand

And struck
The ground

The swirling wind
Folded in upon itself

And revealed
The night

Full with stars.

Occupation

A perfect box of a room, from a bed the view is cropped,
  the world in half

I turn from the window, a vision of movement, to face a T.V void,
  a dark mirror

The door cracks, the sound of male laughter outside,
  then footsteps leaning to silence

I stroke my naked stomach and place a hand on the
  slight ache of my groin

Pulling up my jeans then, pinching the clip of my bra strap then,
  leaving the room then

Wishing for a deeper purpose, a life without continuous exchange

In the corridor a maid smiles and nods at me

I find myself questioning her motives.

More Questions

I went into the forest
and asked -
How long have you been standing here?
What have you seen?
Who have you seen pass by?

Did the boy get the answers he
was looking for when he left
the middle path?

Is he still working his way
through the undergrowth?

Searching for acorns to grow
in his own pots?

Dreaming of high-rises -
whilst living just of a dirt road
near fields and hills.
Full off sheep and tractors cutting lines
and doing turns.

Has he found a clearing yet
to get a good look at the sky?

Or obsessively looking downward?
How often does he look back?

Warn him not to get too involved.

Interview

Name please…
Grass green lion's den
Really?
Yup
Gender?
Squirrel sword with ice cream
No your gender
I just told you
Occupation?
Metal can licker
Please expand on this
Licking metal cans that have been discarded
How is this profitable?
A professional, physically strong bull you say?
Moving on - do you have any allergies?
I have many allies yes, mostly sea turtles and
television characters
No, do you have any adverse affects to anything?
Oh dislikes… hmmm I don't really like frog toes,
but I would never normally mention that
Could you tell me about your strengths?
I can hold up the whole sky with my little finger
of my left hand.

Once

Taking time
In hands that
Do not need it
They age
With restless
Movement

–

That time
Fingertips
In the river
That moved
Beneath
The canoe

–

A cool air
A catch of
Light on water.

Screen Time

One day all your icons will be dead
All your idols will be burnt
Where will you turn
When none of your answers
Are given to you?

Give in now
Let it go

Paint x marks
Quickly over
Photographs
Over portraits of family members
Over past regrets

That way
It's deleted

That way
You cannot be
Considered the prostitute
That you are

When will you appreciate
The sky
For being blue?

Appease the old gods my dear
Let them play
With you
On the water.

Through electric clouds
And perverted smiles
Finish your masterpiece
And let the bastards
Devour it with granite teeth

And don't forget
The burning sword.

Kiki and Ray

Light played with strings
upon her spine.

Man shivered in response
and released the shutter.

Ode to Keith,
AKA The Jazz Man

The girls love that Salsa shite
I f**king hate it.
But the girls they love it.

Salsa music filtering downstairs,
only when the door is open.

Next to the bar
where the woman Dave wants
to marry serves drink after drink -
to students thinking that to understand
jazz you have to listen to it.

And her lips red again
and not really smiling.

Keith never changing,
at least not in mind,
shuts out the North East cold.

Stares at the stragglers outside -
saying you coming in,
with his eyes.

And Keith -
yes I caught him
smile
occasionally -
when the house band
started strong
or the double bass
might have just
vibrated through the old flooring,
causing his lip to
curl up a little.

He's still there you know.
Closing up on Pink Lane,
talking to anyone kind enough
to listen -
late into the night -
leaving in the early morning.

Assigned

Lets take a walk
You and I

I need your help
Well really I would like help
What I'm saying is I'm including
You in the process
Of
Naming
What I've created

What we come across and
What is brought before you
Will be named

You will give
Names to all

Feel the quills
Brush them gently with
Your hands

Tap the shells
And watch the slow movements

Tangle your fingers in
The fur, feel the heat
Of heartbeats, let them
Vibrate into your inner
Being

Smell the salt upon
Arching backs
Of silver of colours
Beyond imagination

Inspect the teeth
The sizes of which and the shapes
Of which are endless

Quicker now
Did you witness
That?

What is that?

It flew across
The sky

Look deeper
Than before into their
Eyes
You will find
You and I reflected in
Them

All earth
Moves and sways
Tell me my loved one
What are the names?

Lastly

When I’m ready to die,
leave me with my thoughts.

Don’t try to put me in a holding place.
Don’t try to keep me locked in
for really your safety.

When I’m ready to go,
let me be what it is I was
and what it is I am.
I’ll be judged accordingly
when I next wake up.

If you have to
be active In the process -
set out the chair,
give me a good view.

Kiss me perhaps upon the cheek
and say what it is you
need to, whether good or bad.

Don’t forget to not say goodbye
because goodbyes do not exist.

Don’t forget to smile because that’s how
I’ll meet you next.

When I’m ready -
I’ll be waiting
in the place of promise.

Art

You were the paint
And I was your painting
Such a disaster

See the cold rivers
See the cold streams
Be the cold nightmare
Be the cold dream

Such is the bloodbath
Call out their names
Insert the poppies
Where else but the veins

Catch the cold quickly
Draw in the night
Sketch what your thinking

Will it be right?

To the Ground

I forgot the sound of
the drums of my ancestors.
The reason for their songs -
- Why they lived?
- How they died?

I put my equipment
to one side
and tried
to find a patch of untainted
earth.

I placed my hands
upon the surface.
Dragged my fingers through dust.
Pleaded with the creator,
with nonsense talk,
whilst hiding electricity
in my back pocket.

I was struck by a line of light.
It blew white
and rumbled out
my lies.

I realised my clothes
were still on
and so tore them to pieces
and pledged to always
be naked.

My face pressed
in, breathing dirt
down my throat and nostrils.

Now, only now,
I hear the beginnings of
a new beat.

Learning Again

With a mind full of totem poles
and hands covered in arrows -

I try to run.

But the sun has drained all
that was left of me -

and the sun decides
which fires to light

and what evenings to kill

and what books to decay

-

In shallow back alley graves -

my knees have been replaced
with the skulls
of our forefathers.

Their mouths
tightly fastened
by nettles and
concrete.

How can I run under circumstances like these?

Where dreams are stored in museum draws
or bought and nailed -
to a rich man's walls.

Perhaps now I must learn to walk again.

Now I must break my paintbrushes -

and now I can crucify the past.

All Through

Corrugated iron glad rusting shacks
Higgledy-piggledy on the river banks
Rows of uncontrollable growing vegetation
All about the situation

Flowing past in scrap car blurring
Not touchable through convex windows
Only imagine the one black cat purring
Rotting compost by the bin loads

Sound is stunted - silence almost has its victory

Under highways seeking hidden ditches
Skulking out of sight wood witches
Another event without eventfulness
A moment in time to forget
Day is bright but activity is dullness
Another meeting with no one met.

How to get on well
during the Digital Revolution

Become an attractive
young woman.

Get attention and gain
followers and…

…make money by
being a
brand and…

…sell yourself,
whatever it takes.

Sell your mind, body
and soul.

Holiday

You hold the stars in a dress,
I'll hold the medicine bags.

I guess this is being wrapped in blue.

Tonight, it's like, a film.
No one knows what happens next.

I guess this is being wrapped in blue.

We were just kids,
painting rocks,
listening to the wind.

Being wrapped in blue.

Write

I look at the blinds in my front room.
They're white and worn.

The sun tries to get through them -
it almost makes it.

My pen sits in a wooden pot.
My computer waits.

Sensitive

I sense the leaves are
falling in the dark.

I know the eyes are
slowly warming up.

If you catch a
glimpse of home.

Give me a call.

I'll come running
through it all.

Contacting Aliens
(Previously published in *erbacce;* 2019)

Step 1
In a pair find an old battered portable television

Step 2
Dismantle the set into
All individual parts
Make sure that all the wires
Are visible

Step 3
Screw and hammer parts together to form a new
Alien seeking device
Add any other necessary
Broken electronic devices
Including an oversized aerial
And a phone with chord attached

Step 4
Attach a musical keyboard and recording equipment
For example a portable tape player
And metal band headphones

Step 5
Plan a day – preferably one in which no sane person would
Want to be outside in
Torrential rain and strong winds
Recommended
Set up equipment under cover of golf umbrella

Step 6
In your pair be excited
By the fuzzing and popping and visual and musical
Recordings you receive from outer space

Step 7
Keep the findings top secret
On a cassette
Don't bother telling the authorities
Or other relatives who wouldn't understand
That you have contacted aliens.

It's Happening Now

Rats follow the notes
of the pipe.

Happily they fall
from the cliff.

The musician
tucks the instrument
into a pocket…

…and walks back inland.

Another Day

'Think of the money'
says dad

'What money?'
says son

Turbulent years follow.

Japanese Celebrity

In words you hide
Pieces of your soul
For all to read

Your name is famous
Yet your face is not.

Industrialisation

Hundreds of fingers
whirling, whizzing, clicking and untangling.

Hundreds of windowsills,
gathering up their own dust.

Personal minds working -
independently from their cotton spinning
machinery.

Waiting for the end of the thirteen hour shift
and looking towards hundreds
of sets of thirteen hour shifts.

Nature First

A naked foot
protrudes from
beneath the roots
of a tree.

An empty hand
stays upright
against the sky.

Give Us One

The brick got tossed.
My hand cradled the gift,
avoiding its sharp edges.

Into the air I watched it leave me
and arch across the white flooded site.
The window dissolved into reflected light.

We all smiled on top of the gravel mound
and carried on searching for
stones in the dark.

Indoors

Knots in the floorboard
create monsters with open fanged mouths
and odd shaped eyes.
They slither and move when no one is watching

and they stay still when they're noticed.

They relish the dull light that works its path through high-
bricked windows.

They never pray for a new dwelling,
just thrive on the misery of new occupants.

Next Sojourn

Please allow
This
Path
To hurt
The
Soles
Of my
Feet.

Which way now?
(Previously published in *erbacce;* 2019)

There's nothing you can teach me
That I don't already know
There's nowhere you can send me
That I wouldn't want to go
There's only one line of defence
But it's only made of snow
I gave so much to dig the trench
Yet there's nothing here to show

Give the word and I'll get over
The next incoming tide
I'll leave the bags and all the lies
That I used to hide
I'll even watch the old town burn
Your star is my guide
Better still I'll avert my eyes
And hold on to your side

There's so much to be written
So much to be read
Got letters from ancient tombstones
Rattling round my head

There's no use moving forward
Dragging behind the dead
But first of all you know me
I best get out of bed

If self belief was in pill form
In any corner shop
Still probably wouldn't take it
Their buying has to stop
I never was on board with it
I only wear a top
To keep the northern chill off
Catch no grief from any cop

The journey has not started
The plans were drawn up before time
The sticky touch of biro ink
Makes me think of the oily line
That appeared as light blinding
So pure, so unrefined
To set off now is impatient
Should I wait for a sign?

Create

I didn't like the world
I was living in

So I imagined
A new one.

Final Thought

I thought of everything
all at once.

I am the universe.